W9-BSU-806

ATLANTA-FULTON PUBLIC LIBRARY

ATLANTA-FULTON PUBLIC LIBRARY

NDEBELE

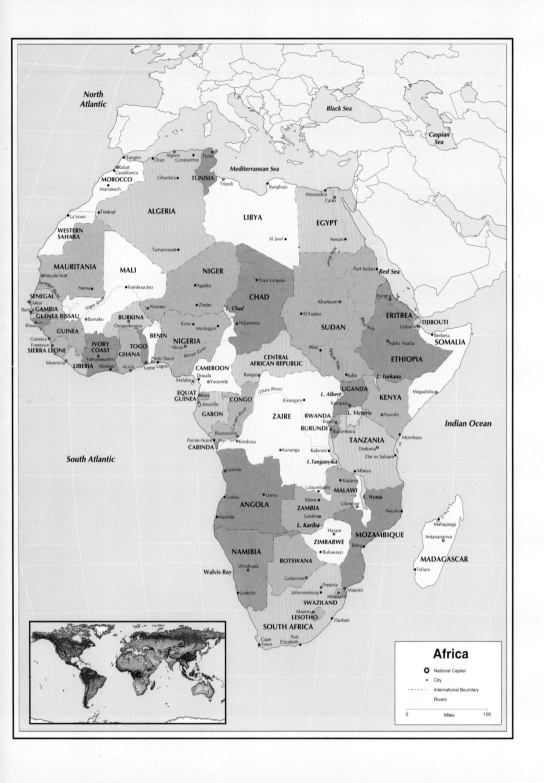

North
Atlantic

Black Sea

Caspian
Sea

Tangier
Algiers
Oran Constantine
Tunis
Rabat
Casablanca
MOROCCO
Ghardaia
TUNISIA
Mediterranean Sea
Tripoli
Marrakech
Banghazi
Alexandria
Cairo

La'youn
Tindouf
ALGERIA
LIBYA
EGYPT

WESTERN
SAHARA
Tamanrasset
Al Jawf
Aswan

MAURITANIA
MALI
NIGER
Faya-Largeau
Port Sudan
Red Sea

Nouakchott
Nema
Tombouctou
Agadez
Asmera

Senegal River
Niger River
Zinder
CHAD
Khartoum
ERITREA
DJIBOUTI

SENEGAL
Niamey
L. Chad
El Fasher
Djibouti
Berbera

Dakar
BURKINA
Kano
Ndjamena
SUDAN
Addis Ababa
SOMALIA

Banjul GAMBIA
Bamako
Ouagadougou
Maiduguri
Wau
ETHIOPIA

GUINEA BISSAU
BENIN
NIGERIA
CENTRAL
White Nile
L. Turkana

Bissau
Conakry
GUINEA
Abuja
Benue River
AFRICAN REPUBLIC
Juba

Freetown
TOGO
GHANA
CAMEROON
Bangui
UGANDA
Mogadishu

SIERRA LEONE
IVORY
COAST
Porto Novo
Douala
L. Albert
KENYA

Monrovia
Abidjan
Accra
Lagos
Yaounde
Kisangani
Kampala

LIBERIA
Lome
EQUAT
GUINEA
Bata
CONGO
(Zaire River)
RWANDA
L. Victoria
Nairobi

Libreville
GABON
ZAIRE
Kigali
Mombasa

CONGO River
Brazzaville
BURUNDI
Bujumbura
TANZANIA

Pointe-Noire
Kinshasa
Kananga
Kalemie
Dodoma
Dar es Salaam

CABINDA
L.Tanganyika
Mbeya

Luanda
Kasama

Indian Ocean

South Atlantic
Lobito
Luena
Lubumbashi
MALAWI
L. Nyasa

ANGOLA
Kitwe
Lilongwe
Nacala

Namibe
ZAMBIA
Lusaka
L. Kariba
Harare
MOZAMBIQUE

ZIMBABWE
Beira
MADAGASCAR

NAMIBIA
Bulawayo
Mahajanga

BOTSWANA
Antananarivo

Walvis Bay
Windhoek
Gaborone
Pretoria
Maputo
Toliara

Luderitz
Johannesburg
Mbabane

SWAZILAND
Maseru
LESOTHO
Durban

SOUTH AFRICA

Cape
Town
Port
Elizabeth

Africa

✪ National Capital
• City
------ International Boundary
—— Rivers

0   Miles   100

The Heritage Library of African Peoples

NDEBELE

Elizabeth Ann Schneider, Ph.D.

THE ROSEN PUBLISHING GROUP, INC.
NEW YORK

Published in 1997 by The Rosen Publishing Group, Inc.
29 East 21st Street, New York, NY 10010

Copyright 1997 by The Rosen Publishing Group, Inc.

All rights reserved. No part of this book may be reproduced in any form without permission in writing from the publisher, except by a reviewer.

First Edition

Manufactured in the United States of America

Library of Congress Cataloging-in-Publication Data

Schneider, Elizabeth Ann
    Ndebele / Elizabeth Ann Schneider. — 1st ed.
        p.   cm. — (The heritage library of African peoples)
    Includes bibliographical references and index.
    ISBN 0-8239-2009-7
    1. Ndebele (African people)—Juvenile literature.   I. Title.
II. Series.
DT1768.N42S35   1996
968'.00496398—dc20   96-20758
                                                                                          CIP
                                                                                          AC

Contents

INTRODUCTION

THERE IS EVERY REASON FOR US TO KNOW something about Africa and to understand its past and the way of life of its peoples. Africa is a rich continent that has for centuries provided the world with art, culture, labor, wealth, and natural resources. It has vast mineral deposits, fossil fuels, and commercial crops.

But perhaps most important is the fact that fossil evidence indicates that human beings originated in Africa. The earliest traces of human beings and their tools are almost two million years old. Their descendants have migrated throughout the world. To be human is to be of African descent.

The experiences of the peoples who stayed in Africa are as rich and as diverse as of those who established themselves elsewhere. This series of books describes their environment, their modes of subsistence, their relationships, and their customs and beliefs. The books present the variety of languages, histories, cultures, and religions that are to be found on the African continent. They demonstrate the historical linkages between African peoples and the way contemporary Africa has been affected by European colonial rule.

Africa is large, complex, and diverse. It encompasses an area of more than 11,700,000 square miles. The United States, Europe, and India could fit easily into it. The sheer size is an indication of the continent's great variety in geography, terrain, climate, flora, fauna, peoples, languages, and cultures.

Much of contemporary Africa has been shaped by European colonial rule, industrialization, urbanization, and the demands of a world economic system. For more than seventy years, large regions of Africa were ruled by Great Britain, France, Belgium, Portugal, and Spain. African peoples from various ethnic, linguistic, and cultural backgrounds were brought together to form colonial states.

For decades Africans struggled to gain their independence. It was not until after World War II that the colonial territories became independent African states. Today, almost all of Africa is ruled by Africans. Large numbers of Africans live in modern cities. Rural Africa is also being transformed, and yet its people still engage in many of their customs and beliefs.

Contemporary circumstances and natural events have not always been kind to ordinary Africans. Today, however, new popular social movements and technological innovations pose great promise for future development.

George C. Bond, Ph.D., Director
Institute of African Studies
Columbia University, New York

The Ndebele are famous for their beautiful beadwork, which helps identify a person's status. This woman's outfit, for special occasions, includes a married woman's apron and a heavily beaded blanket. Her hat and neck rings are seen in detail on the cover of this book.

PREFACE

SOUTHERN AFRICA HAS BEEN TRANSFORMED
by the dramatic arrival of democracy in South
Africa, the last African country to emerge from
colonial and cultural domination and minority
rule. The world watched in wonder as the elec-
tions of 1994 peacefully concluded South
Africa's long quest for freedom. South Africa's
new constitution and bill of rights, arguably the
most progressive in the world, are a high point
in African and world history.

Now southern African scholars are finally free
to present their history, their rich heritage, and
the heroic efforts their peoples have made. There
is a wide audience eager for these truths that
have been distorted and silenced for so long.
The timely Heritage Library of African Peoples
series on southern Africa can play an invaluable
role in cementing people's appreciation of their
own heritage; in fostering understanding among
all the peoples of the region; and in sharing with
readers worldwide the unique and fascinating
cultures of southern Africa.

As a Mosotho and a southern African, I
wholeheartedly welcome this insightful book and
the southern African series.

T. T. Thahane, Deputy Governor
of the South African Reserve Bank;
former Vice President of the World Bank.

Many rural Ndebele, such as this woman from Kinross, paint beautiful, geometric murals on their houses. This art form is a proud sign of Ndebele culture, and it has become popular with tourists. Today, Ndebele designs are copied all over the world.

1

THE PEOPLE

THE NDEBELE, PARTICULARLY THE
Ndzundza Ndebele (pronounced zund-za en-DEH-bel-eh) of South Africa, are a proud, artistic people. They have become world famous for their colorful beadwork, traditional dress, and unique wall paintings. They are also known for their tragic history and admired for their ability to survive defeat. Few people realize that there is a connection between their artistic wall painting and beadwork and their history.

The Ndzundza live mostly on the Highveld, a high, grassland plateau in the northeast part of South Africa. The region where they live is now known as Mpumalanga. It lies next to Swaziland and Mozambique. In April 1994, when South Africa finally became a democratic country, some of its provinces (states) were renamed. Formerly, Mpumalanga was the eastern part of a much larger province called the Transvaal.

LANGUAGE AND THE NAME "NDEBELE"

Why are these people called Ndebele? They may have been called "Ndebele" because of their language. It was quite different from the language spoken by their neighbors. The Ndebele spoke the language of the Nguni people, who lived near the northeast coast of present-day South Africa. When some early Ndebele moved into the eastern Transvaal in the 1800s, they were surrounded by people who spoke the Sotho language. The Sotho noted the different language and customs of the Ndebele. They referred to the Ndebele as strangers from the east, or Matebele. This was the name they gave to all Nguni-speaking foreigners. Gradually it was changed into Ndebele, the Nguni form of the word.

There are a few South African groups who call themselves Ndebele, but they belong to separate societies and have different histories. These Ndebele groups distinguish themselves by adding a famous chief's name to their group name, such as "Ndzundza" Ndebele. The various Ndebele chiefdoms all share a Nguni heritage.

However, only the Ndzundza Ndebele decorate their homesteads so colorfully and wear such unusual traditional dress. This book refers to these Ndebele people.

Today, numerous Ndebele live in the large cities of South Africa, but the many Ndebele in the rural areas continue to follow their traditions.

Much of the Highveld has an elevation of more than 5,000 feet above sea level. The air is brisk and the climate healthy. There is plenty of sunshine and relatively little rainfall. Highveld summers are hot. Fierce rain and thunderstorms often beat down on the land. Winter,

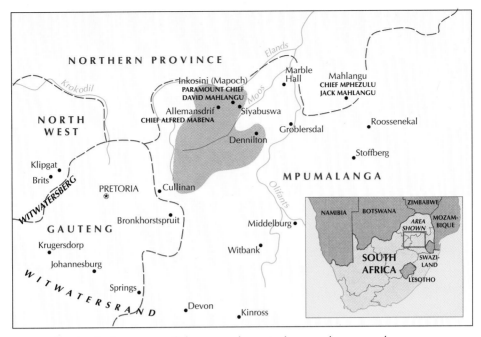

The shaded portion of the map above indicates the area where most rural Ndebele live today. Many other Ndebele live in large towns and cities such as Pretoria and Johannesburg.

even though it is usually sunny, can be bitterly cold. Temperatures often fall below freezing, especially at night. The winters are dry.

In winter, the rural Ndebele woman finds a sheltered, sunny spot, close to the homestead wall, to do her chores. Here she sorts ground-nuts, dries wild spinach, and does her beadwork. Winter is also the time to repair the earthen walls of the houses and the outdoor courtyard where people spend much of their time. To repair her courtyard, a woman smears the packed earth with cattle dung and water. This mixture sets hard like cement. Chemicals in the dung kill bugs and germs. Patterns are often drawn in the wet clay floor. After the surface dries, it is polished. The walls are very carefully painted.

13

In the past, people measured their wealth in cattle, which were an important part of their culture. Today, few Ndebele have cattle, even though many Ndebele still live in rural areas. Most rural Ndebele live and work on white people's farms as migrant tenant laborers. The term "tenant laborer" means that the Ndebele families live, as well as work, on those farms. The word migrant means that they live there temporarily, usually for a few years, and then they must move on. Until recently, white farmers or the previous government could force tenant laborers off the farms at any time. Because this life was so difficult and insecure, many Ndebele tried to get permits to move to the towns and cities or commuted many hours to work there.

Today, rural Ndebele men help white farmers plow, plant, and harvest corn, one of the main crops in Mpumalanga. The women work for the farmers' wives in the farmhouse, or they labor in the fields. When the young children become old enough they, too, help in the fields or in the house.

Until recently, the pay for farmworkers was very low: a few sacks of cornmeal and a little cash. To supplement farmworkers' income, the farmer lends tenants a small plot on the farm so they can build a home and grow food to eat. Tenant families usually keep chickens and some-times a goat or other livestock.

The South African government created an Ndebele village as a tourist attraction to promote Ndebele arts. These women in ceremonial dresses are posing for photographers.

Ndebele homesteads are quite different from those of their neighbors. Their Sotho-speaking neighbors live in houses that are sometimes decorated in earth-tone colors. These homes quietly blend into the earth on which they rest. By contrast, the houses of the Ndebele are colorfully decorated. They use strong black lines in their striking patterns. The reason the Ndebele began to paint their earthen homesteads in this unusual way is linked to their history.▲

chapter

2

EARLY HISTORY

THE NDEBELE PEOPLE HAVE A STRONG sense of identity and pride. While this is true of many African peoples, it is especially true among the Ndzundza Ndebele. They have had a troubled history, yet they find great strength in remembering their past. They recall how strong their ancestors had to be when white settlers waged war against them in 1883.

During the 1860s, the Ndzundza Ndebele were one of the most powerful chiefdoms in the Transvaal. They lived in strong rock fortresses in the mountains that made it almost impossible for an enemy to challenge them. Their land was vast, and they had many cattle grazing upon it. The earth in their gardens was so fertile that they are said to have grown peaches the size of papayas. They also produced the best grass to thatch roofs for miles around.

At this time, white settlers began to arrive.

Many Ndebele today live in small villages on white-owned farms in the Mpumalanga province. Conditions are poor. The girls above are walking from their houses to the nearest water source.

They were known as Boers, a Dutch word meaning "farmers," or Afrikaners, meaning Dutch settlers who had been born in Africa. South Africa was first colonized by the Dutch, who settled in Cape Town in 1652. Later, the British took control from the Dutch. Many Boers refused to be ruled by the British. They moved away from the Cape Colony and into the interior of South Africa. There they began to settle on land owned by African peoples like the Ndebele. In 1856 the Boers declared their own independent republic, called the South African Republic (SAR), later named the Transvaal.

The Ndebele's power was so great that the Boers paid them yearly rent for letting their cattle graze on Ndzundza land. The white farmers wanted to take Ndebele land and cattle, but they found that the chiefdom was too powerful to challenge directly. However, a violent event in a

neighboring chiefdom provided the Boers with their opportunity.

Mampuru, a royal member of a neighboring Sotho chiefdom, murdered his chief. He hoped to gain the throne for himself. However, his people were so angry that he had to flee to the Ndzundza Ndebele for temporary shelter. The Sotho people and the Boers of the SAR wanted to punish Mampuru. The Ndebele, however, refused to give him up. Legend says that the Ndebele chief said, "I can't give him to you. I've swallowed him into my stomach." This refusal, plus the chance of gaining Ndebele land, gave the SAR government an excuse to attack the Ndzundza Ndebele, with Sotho help. They fought a bitter war that lasted for almost a year.

The SAR government used powerful guns against the Ndebele and tried to blast the rock fortress. They also surrounded the fortress and cut off the Ndebele food supply. But the Ndebele mountain fortresses with their many caves remained firm against this siege. Some caves had large rooms where the Ndebele families lived; there was a plentiful supply of water. There was even one special cave for women and children. But as time went on, food became scarce.

Because the Ndebele were cut off from their planted fields, many people died of starvation. In desperation, they were forced to surrender after many months of hunger. The SAR government had won that war. As punishment, SAR officials condemned the Ndebele chief and Mampuru to death. The other Ndzundza Ndebele royals were sentenced to many years of hard labor.

Later, the death sentence was changed to life imprisonment for the Ndebele chief. Mampuru, however, was hanged, and the Ndebele chief was forced to watch. The government forced the rest of the Ndzundza population—some 10,000 people—to become indentured laborers for five years. This meant they had to work on the farms of the Afrikaners. The Ndzundza Ndebele people were scattered onto Afrikaner farms all over the former Transvaal.

The Ndzundza chief was released from prison when he began having health problems. The Ndzundza community then collected money to buy a farm where they could gather together as a nation again. It took years. Each family contributed an ox to pay for it. Gradually this group located the farms where other Ndzundza Ndebele lived and worked, and the people reunited.

Though defeated in war, the people never lost their pride. The ordeal had made them deeply aware and proud of their Ndzundza Ndebele identity.▲

3

HOMESTEAD
DECORATION

THE NDEBELE FEELING OF UNITY WAS strengthened by a new tradition—homestead decoration. They wanted to distinguish their homesteads from those of their Sotho neighbors.

In the 1940s, some Ndebele women began to decorate the outside mud walls of their homesteads. They made whitewashed outlines of the walls, doors, and windows; they added small designs to the blank spaces. They used colored earth or powdered pigment from the trading store. This was mixed with clay, cooked cornmeal, and cattle dung so the designs would withstand the harsh summer rains.

One Ndebele community created such unusual designs that an architect took his students to photograph the farm settlement each year as the designs changed. When the farm was sold, the architect suggested that the government relocate the families and create an Ndebele

Ndebele women often decorate both the walls and the courtyard floor of their homestead (above). Below, Christina Skosana, whose family works on a farm near Devon in Mpumalanga, creates her annual home decoration. Many murals have geometric designs that are similar to those in Ndebele beadwork. Today, there are many different styles of Ndebele painting.

Bright commercial paints were available to some Ndebele painters. They developed a very colorful style of mural art that is popular today (above and opposite). The designs often include recognizable objects, such as the jet above, which may have been inspired by the planes from a nearby air base.

tourist village near Pretoria. This they did, providing paint for the houses and thatch for the roofing. They charged tourists a fee to enter the village and take pictures. The Ndebele families responded by creating a colorful village. This inspired Ndebele women in other villages and farms to try to outdo the decorations at the tourist village.

The wives of Ndebele laborers who lived and worked on white men's farms were poorer than those living in chiefdoms or villages. They had to find less expensive ways to decorate. Often, they walked for miles to find colored earth deposits that could be used as paint. For additional colors they used bluing (a blue laundry powder), shoe polish, and red or green floor wax. They created the color black from soot, river soil, or water-soaked flashlight batteries.

A white flag is flown outside houses that will be hosting an important celebration.

Later, some women began painting their decorations with acrylic paint. These manufactured paints are brighter and last longer against the rains than most natural dyes, but they are expensive.

The Ndebele house designs were similar to those used in Ndebele beadwork. Traditionally, the Ndebele beaded their goatskin aprons and blankets. Other designs were inspired by patterns on cloth or designs on linoleum floors. The women decorators used whatever shapes looked interesting to them. Some designs featured an attractive building or sights seen on a trip to town. The patterns soon came to be painted in a distinctively angular, geometric way that was called "Ndebele style." By painting their homes in this way, the people were proudly displaying their Ndebele identity and heritage.

For celebrations, it was important for the

23

women to paint fresh decorations to welcome the many friends and relatives who came to visit. A white flag was flown from a tall pole in front of houses to announce a celebration—such as a graduation, a wedding, or a new baby's arrival.

Tourists from Johannesburg and other centers began to drive out to see these colorful Ndebele homesteads. The Ndebele women noticed the license plates on the cars. Although they could not read the plates, they liked the shapes of the various letters and numbers and began to paint them on their earthen walls. They used the letters and numbers as mirror images of each other, making symmetrical patterns. These were used on the front of the house or on the exterior of the walls that often surrounded Ndebele homesteads.

As the painting custom grew, women competed with one another to create more elaborate designs. Some patterns featured airplanes like those that flew overhead from the nearby air base. The decorations in the chief's village were particularly colorful, as if announcing that it was the Ndzundza Ndebele capital. But the village where the designs originated became the most elaborate of all.

Ndebele women are sometimes asked why they work so hard each year to decorate their walls, especially when the summer rains wash

The house and its decoration are the responsibility of women. Some women include sculptures on the outer walls of their homestead courtyard. The figures of married women, above, were made by a schoolteacher to decorate her parents' home.

away the designs. They reply that the designs let people know that Ndebele people are living there—that it is their custom. These unique homesteads, which brighten the dust-colored landscape in Mpumalanga, allow one to identify a Ndzundza Ndebele homestead immediately.

The art of the Ndzundza Ndebele is closely connected to their history. Their sufferings brought out their strong sense of identity, and this identity is celebrated for the world to see through Ndebele art.▲

chapter

4

YOUTH ACTIVITIES

▼ BOYS' ACTIVITIES ▼

Young Ndebele boys living in the country-side discover and learn many things. They spread sticky insect wax on tree branches and fence wires to trap birds, or kill them with sling-shots. Bird feathers are valuable and are worn for special ceremonies.

A work crew of boys, *igwabo*, is sent by the king into the bush to catch a red falcon for the ceremony called Luma, the Feast of First Fruits. The falcon must not be harmed during the capture. The falcon is needed so the king can wear its feathers during the Luma celebration. At the ceremony, the king takes the first bite of the year's pumpkin crop. No one can eat from the first harvest until the king has *luma* (bitten) the pumpkin. After he tastes it, the other family heads also taste it. At the Luma feast, a heaven-bird feather, the red feather normally worn by the king, is burned as part of the ceremony.

Ndebele boys make creative wire toys with working parts. This car has wheels made from empty snuff containers.

▼ PLAY ▼

Ndebele boys use wire to construct toy cars, trucks, airplanes, bicycles, sewing machines, and even animals. These are very inventive toys with working parts. It is clear that the boys carefully study the workings of the machines upon which their toys are based.

The small wire cars are about a foot long. They have snuff cans for wheels and long steering columns that reach up to the boys' chests. This allows the boys to steer the car as they run behind it. The boys often hold car races, creating dust clouds behind them.

Their miniature sewing machines have a wire needle that moves up and down with the

27

turn of a wire handwheel. This imitates the motion of the old-fashioned, hand-turned sewing machines that they often see. Ndebele wire bicycles, ranging from seven to ten inches long, have handlebars, wheels, and pedals that actually turn.

A favorite game is played in a circle with a tennis ball. The object of the game is to pass the ball around the circle without using your hands and without letting it hit the ground. The boys use their heads, knees, and feet to control the ball. These coordination skills are good training for other sports like soccer.

▼ GIRLS' ACTIVITIES ▼

Girls also make their own toys. They make dolls from cloth and sticks, and carry them in a sling across their backs the way that Ndebele mothers carry their babies. Girls often make imaginary homesteads by placing stones on the ground to outline rooms and doorways.

One of the chores girls perform is feeding the chickens. They often enjoy creating their own tiny chickens from wet clay. To make her fowl seem more real, a girl uses beads for eyes and presses more beads onto the wings before the clay hardens.

When girls are a little older, they learn to use beadwork to decorate the traditional clothes that are worn on special occasions. Decorating the

A beaded doll, usually made by their mothers, is sometimes worn by young girls as part of their ceremonial dress (above). Girls also wear a small beaded front apron (*phephetu*) and a towel over their hips.

homestead becomes their responsibility when they reach puberty. For girls, those decorations are a special treat. They can create their own designs and create whatever appeals to them. However, everyone expects the designs to be done in the Ndebele style.▲

chapter

5

CUSTOMS

▼ PRAISE POEMS ▼

Ndebele society and other South African societies have a special way of sharing the history of a chiefdom, a family, or an individual. It is an art form called praise poetry, *izibongo*. *Izibongo* has been handed down for centuries. Reciting praise poems reminds listeners of the Ndebele nation's history and important events that happened under certain chiefs. Sometimes these poems can be witty as well.

There are several kinds of *izibongo*. The most important one is the *izibongo* of the royal family—the official history of the chiefdom. Then there is the ordinary family's *izibongo*, which every Ndebele family has. All of the men must learn their family's *izibongo*, which is not, of course, as long as the royal family's praise poem. Finally, there is an individual's *izibongo*, which is even shorter.

Poems are recited like songs. Royal praises are sung at important official gatherings by an honored praise singer called an *imbongi*. Before the ceremony begins, he recites the praises. This takes fifteen or twenty minutes and is done at a particular tempo and pitch of voice. He pauses between each chief's name and then chants the noteworthy events that occurred under that chief, using a poetic pattern of words. As he chants, he gestures with his *ubhutshulo* (a four-foot-long stick with ostrich feathers at the top) to place emphasis on each fact.

The singer reminds the audience of the time when the Ndebele were a powerful chiefdom. He recalls earlier times when white settlers paid tribute for permission to graze cattle on Ndebele land, and when Ndebele warriors were victorious.

As the praise singer pauses, the men thump their sticks and shout: "*Ehe!*" in agreement, which means "Yes!" To show their approval, women, make loud, high-pitched sounds by using their tongues and lips.

When the singer begins to describe the Ndebele defeat in the 1883 war with the Afrikaners, the men sigh sadly and the women wail. He reminds the audience of the cruel siege laid against the Ndebele and how they starved. The community's bitter history during the war of 1883 and its aftermath are recalled. The audience remembers that its chief was imprisoned and that Ndzundza society was broken up. However, praise poems always end by reminding people how their proud Ndzundza nation overcame disaster and regained strength.

The retelling of events through praises is sometimes unclear to outsiders. The references to the past are sometimes understood only by fellow Ndzundza. The oral poet Vilakazi describes the praises as "emotional shorthand."

▼ TRADITIONAL DRESS ▼

The women's traditional dress has always been much more colorful than that of the men. Women's clothing is decorated with elaborate beadwork. Over the years, Ndebele women have become famous for such beadwork. A woman's traditional apron shows the stage of life that she is in. When she graduates from one stage to another, for example, from being newly married to becoming a mother, the change is shown by alterations in her dress.

Beaded patterns are sewn onto the blankets that women wear over their shoulders on special occasions. On these gala days, a woman also wears her finest beaded apron, and additional beaded bracelets and leg rings.

Copper and brass neck, arm, and leg rings used to be a basic part of the everyday dress of rural Ndebele. Now, they are generally only worn for special occasions. They are heated and

The clothing of senior women is always the most colorful. These women wear many traditional items. The long strips hanging down from their heads are worn by women with initiated sons. Notice the beaded staff held below the blanket of the woman on the left.

THE CHANGING ART OF TRADITIONAL DRESS

Today, Ndebele dress still reflects the different stages of life, but there have been changes in how the Ndebele women make their clothing.

Traditional aprons and blankets are beaded, but such materials have become expensive. Some women now substitute new plastic material for the blanket and skin aprons. Showing creativity, they sew on cloth trims and colored bias tape, or narrow strip of cloth, in zigzag and symmetrical patterns. It is a thrifty replacement for costly beads. The shape of the plastic apron and its flaps still indicate a woman's status: unmarried, bride, or married woman. Some blankets are now decorated with colorful handkerchiefs, small mirrors, plastic ornaments, and even toy handcuffs. A yarn message might be embroidered on a cloth scarf worn over a woman's shoulders.

Today, women's neck and leg rings still look like metal, but they are made from flexible strips of silver-colored plastic bought from car supply stores. Buttons and loops are now attached so the rings can be easily removed. Women still wear thick, beaded grass hoops, but now have colored electrical tape and thumbtacks worked into the pattern. Thus, the artwork has changed to fit the present situation.

Another reason for the change is that Ndebele beadwork has become valuable in the tourist and art world. The women sell their old aprons and blankets because they need the money. They replace them by making newer and cheaper ones that perform the same functions. Whether Ndebele dress is made of skin, wool, or plastic, with beads or other ornaments, it is still a powerful way of stating Ndebele identity.

These women model two different kinds of a married woman's apron. The skin apron on the left is decorated with beads, while the one on the right is made from inexpensive cloth, plastic, and tape. Instead of traditional brass leg rings, both women wear rings made from plastic auto trim. The girl on the right is wearing her school uniform.

shaped right on a woman's body. Metal neck rings indicate that a woman is married. Larger beaded hoops fit loosely over the metal neck rings. A knitted cap, or some head covering, usually in blue—a favorite color of the Ndebele, is worn. When dancing, or in a procession, a woman holds a decorated dancing mace or staff as well. Today, it may be a beaded flashlight.

The front apron that a woman wears for galas is made of goat skin and is elaborately decorated with beads of many colors. A bride's apron has five rounded flaps on the bottom. A married woman's apron has two square flaps with a beaded fringe in between. The back apron is plain, but may include metal rings for decoration. By using both brass and copper rings, a woman can be creative with her back apron.

Very young children wear a *ghabi*. It is a tiny,

Ndebele women wear their finest dress when attending the graduation ceremony for male and female initiates (above left). This woman (above right) has embroidered her address on her back to remind her fiancé, who is working far away, to write to her.

stiff piece of canvas that ties around the hips, and has a beaded fringe. At celebrations, young girls from the ages of three to thirteen wear a *phephetu*. This is a larger, rigid, rectangular canvas apron with beaded designs sewn onto it. Across the back of their hips they wrap a colorful towel.

▼ GIRLS' INITIATION ▼

At puberty (around age fourteen), a young girl goes through an individual initiation ceremony in her mother's home. Here, she receives instruction from her mother and older women in private, and she does not go out. During this period of isolation, the older women teach her

Relatives of a girl initiate wear their finest beaded blankets for her coming-out ceremony (above left). The principal wife of Chief Mphezulu Jack Mahlangu holds one of her children. Alongside is another of his three wives.

the rules and responsibilities of a young bride. These include having respect for elders and being a good wife. She must honor her husband. She is told secrets that she must not reveal to anyone else. Then she is joined by several of her friends who were initiated the previous year. They sing special satirical songs. They learn the words of *hlonipha*, a secret language of their own.

The initiate may not drink *amasi* (thick milk) and must not be touched. At this time she is taught how to decorate the walls of her homestead. The isolation lasts for one month, during which the initiate wears thick, beaded grass rings on her waist and legs to indicate her status. At the end of this period of isolation, she goes to the river with her friends and completely washes herself.

The girls sing as they return. The initiate walks slowly among them, her head covered with an old blanket. It signifies that she is leaving her childhood and old ways. She will be welcomed with a new blanket indicating the beginning of her new life. Then, a joyful welcoming ceremony begins.

All of the female relatives, dressed in their finest, bring gifts. The older women make an impressive, dignified entrance into the courtyard. Walking in single file, the older women carry gifts of blankets, gourd dishes, and mats carefully balanced on their heads. Forming a circle around the girl, they give her brief words of advice. They then perform a small dance to a clapped rhythm as each gift is given. The girl acknowledges each gift with a few dance steps of her own. This ceremony concludes the young girl's welcome to adulthood. It publicly acknowledges that she is now ready for marriage.

Meanwhile, the men gather to one side, and sit in the shade chatting and drinking home-brewed beer. When the ceremony is finished, a goat for the ceremonial feast is killed when a man delivers a powerful blow to the goat's head with his fist. After the feast of roasted or boiled goat and cornmeal, singing and dancing begin.

▼ BOYS' INITIATION ▼

Initiation, or *ingoma*, is a boy's official transition from youth to manhood. *Ingoma* represents an important rite of passage that affects men for the rest of their lives. Although circumcision is a central part of the initiation, the entire phase is lengthy and involves the whole community. All boys between the ages of fifteen and nineteen are expected to undergo initiation. The process begins once a king's son is ready to go through *ingoma*. There are several stages in the male initiation process.

Ingoma lasts more than four years. During the first stage, the boys work in the king's fields three days a week for four years. While in a work crew, the boys wear their hair in a special style and learn their secret *hlonipha* language. Male *hlonipha* words are useful later when men want to talk to each other privately and not be understood by the uninitiated or by women. Some *hlonipha* words are similar to their normal Ndebele language equivalent. For example, instead of using the word "eyes," they substitute "lookers."

The final stage is completed during an intense two-month period called *wela*. *Wela* means "to go through, or over"; it signifies that the initiates have crossed the river that divides boys from men.

Once they have completed their long work

period, the boys go to the king and ask for *wela*, the final stage of the initiation with all of its rights. They demand the right to be recognized as adults with higher status within the household. They demand the right to contribute to decision-making within Ndebele society, and the right to inherit. Most important of all, they demand their right to marry.

In turn, the king announces that *wela* will begin with the first new moon around early May, at the beginning of South Africa's winter. The moon is often used to coordinate activities throughout the land. At that time, all of the nearby initiates gather in the king's courtyard. Those farther away gather in the courtyard of the headman of their region, where they spend the night. Each boy pays the king a certain amount of money (equivalent to about $10). The next morning, they head into the bush for *wela*, the final two months of initiation training. There, they undergo circumcision.

In addition to circumcision, male initiation includes instruction about men's responsibilities as adults. Men learn the importance of loyalty to the king and royals. They practice masculine arts and undergo rigorous physical tests to show their courage. Individually, they are given new names, and learn *izibongo* (praise poetry). All are warned that they must never reveal the secrets of initiation. Their group is given a special name

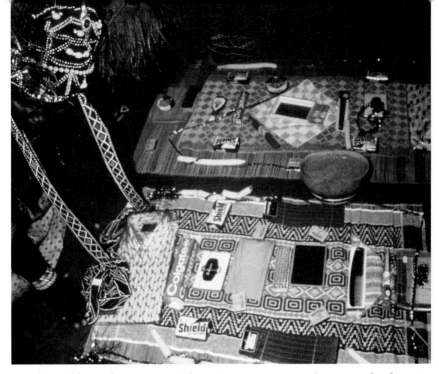

The mother of an initiate (above) sews many graduation gifts from friends and relatives onto a reed mat for her son. Many of the gifts are clothes and items for personal grooming.

that will not be given to another unit for sixty years.

Each initiation school is led by a senior member of the royal class. The total number of people involved is very large. At the initiation held in 1985, there were 190 headmen to supervise the more than 10,000 young men who were initiated.

During their four years together, the young men develop a close bond that lasts their entire lives. They are not allowed to marry until the prince in their age-regiment weds. This occurs about a year after graduation.

After completing this difficult training, initiates are proudly welcomed back into the

Graduates are dressed in fine beadwork made by their girlfriends and families. Each in turn, t
men chant the *izibongo* that they have composed and learned during the initiation school.

community. They are dressed in the beaded clothing that their mothers and girlfriends have made for them. Each young man is presented with many gifts that have been sewn onto bead-fringed mats, which are held up for all to see. The male teacher in charge announces the giver and describes each item: shirts, toothpaste, pants, shaving gear, or soap. The young men give thanks by individually chanting their personal *izibongo* (praises) that they composed while in isolation.

A young man's praises start with announcing his new name. He then describes imaginary challenges and his achievements. One young man dramatically performed his praise poem for a small gift of soap which lay on the mat. In his praises, he vividly described his plans for bathing with the soap before he went driving in his imaginary fancy new car. This spontaneous praise was greeted with hearty laughter; the women howled with approval.

Ingoma is a happy celebration, with women singing and dancing gracefully in traditional dress. Later, younger men display warrior maneuvers, leaping in the air and thumping on their shields with heavy clubs. The older men sit to one side, watching. They wear Western clothing, but some are wearing their *poryana* (animal skin neckpieces or bibs). A *poryana* is worn only by initiated men. It is made of a special animal

skin and often features beaded decorations. There is unlimited drinking of homemade beer for everyone.

Male initiation ceremonies are important within traditional society. A male has little status within his community unless he has undergone the total *ingoma*. If he has not, he is considered a "non-man." This remains true today for most Ndebele young men.

However, a minority of Ndebele men have reservations about the initiation process. The time involved interrupts their school schedule, the long absence can put jobs at risk, and the total *ingoma* ceremony can be very costly. The circumcision itself can be dangerous to men's health. Other men may object to *ingoma* as not being relevant in today's world.

▼ *HLONIPHA*: RESPECT AND ▼ A SECRET LANGUAGE

Two Ndebele customs are very important within traditional society. One is *hlonipha*, which means "to treat with respect" and is also the name of the secret language learned by initiates. The other is *zila*, meaning "to avoid or abstain from." *Hlonipha* behavior is shown by actions and words, or more correctly, by *not* using certain words.

For a young woman, *hlonipha* behavior begins when she becomes engaged and continues until her first child is born. When a bride enters her husband's homestead, she serves an apprenticeship with her mother-in-law. She is watched closely and taught about the family into which she has married. She has to use *hlonipha* in dealing with her in-laws. She must treat them with respect and consideration. A bride cannot use the names of her father-in-law, her husband, or his brothers. She cannot even use words similar to their names. Other words are substituted instead. (However, in urban areas today, women are starting to use the personal names of their husbands.) She may speak to her father-in-law only when absolutely necessary. When doing so, she must cover her face and turn her back. Above all, he must not see her breasts or naked back.

Within the homestead and outside, a young bride must wear a *hlonipha* scarf tied over one shoulder. It shows she is married and is a sign of respect for the homestead. It is believed that the spirits of the ancestors are always present around the homestead and will be offended if they are not shown the proper respect. This could bring sickness or trouble for the family or the bride.

The young wife must also practice *zila*, which means she must not eat certain foods, and she must avoid certain places. Cow's milk is forbidden until she has her first child. The kraal (or corral) where the cattle are kept is forbidden to her. After the wife's first child is born, her father-in-law will formally acknowledge the birth with a celebration and feast. After the feast, some of the restrictions are lifted. Still, she must refrain from using certain names.

When a new bride demonstrates her knowledge of *hlonipha* and *zila* customs, she shows herself to be a well-behaved person. It strengthens her place in the husband's family and shows that she is aware of her social obligations. This also reassures the husband's family that she will not offend the ancestral spirits through ignorance. Doing so would bring the anger of the family gods down on the household and herself.

Only married women beyond their childbearing years can afford to ignore these rules. They have already won respect because of their *hlonipha* behavior.

An Ndebele husband must follow similar restrictions when dealing with his in-laws. He must never use the names of his wife's mother or sister. Other words are substituted instead. The restrictions are partly lifted after two children have been born, with a feast celebrating the occasion.

A number of *hlonipha* requirements are not observed by urban Ndebele women today. However, many are still followed because they are regarded as essential good manners. In the

Ndebele newlyweds must both observe special rules of respect towards their new in-laws. Here, Chief Alfred Mabena (of the Manala section of the Ndebele) and his principal wife perform a repeat of their original wedding ceremony, held many years before. The bridal veil and ostrich-feathered staff are traditional items.

rural parts of the country, they are more important. But it is not unusual to see an Ndebele woman working in the big city of Pretoria wearing a *hlonipha* scarf over one shoulder. She fears her own homestead might suffer sickness or trouble of some sort if she is without it. It would be doubly serious if her husband happened to see her when she was not wearing it.

▼ NAMING ▼

Choosing a child's name is very important. African names can contain more meanings than the names Westerners generally use. African names are formed from primary sources in the language, such as nouns, verbs, and so on. African names can tell us what language is spoken at home, and the gender of the person. Sometimes a name conveys whether a person has brothers and sisters, or whether he or she was born first or last. Often, names indicate important events. The Ndebele feel that names should have positive meanings so that a child will live up to his or her name.

An Ndebele child is named when he or she is about seven months old. An Ndebele girl is usually named by her mother's mother or one of her mother's sisters. The boys are named by their father's fathers or brothers. The naming ceremony of the first child is the most important. The mother presents the new child to the spirits of the ancestors at the first new moon following the birth. Later children are named by their parents, and the names often refer to a significant event that happened near the time of the birth. Naming a child "July" would indicate that an important event happened in that month to inspire the name.

A female child might be called uThimba or uNdazana, both meaning "girl" in the Ndebele language. Sometimes a male child will simply be called uSomfana (meaning "boy"). Usually the name will be more specific. For example, the name uVusumuzi ("he revives the family") is a common male name in Ndebele families, but is used for the firstborn son only.

The names that the Afrikaner farmers gave to the Ndzundza laborers after the 1883 war reveal their prejudices. Rather than trying to pro-nounce difficult African names, the farmers chose another way. On work contracts many Ndebele were called "September" or "January," the month of their contract. Others were called "Swaartbooi" (Afrikaans for "black boy") or "Kleinbooi" (Afrikaans for "small boy") refer-ring to their appearance. Biblical names such as Jonas or Joseph were also popular. The Ndzundza had their names for the white farmers as well. The Ndebele word for "miser" was one of them. Another farmer was called Makethane ("he who hits with a chain").

▼ MANY NAMES FOR ONE PERSON ▼

It is customary in Ndebele society for one person to have several names. One is the "home name," a traditional, personal name given shortly after birth. That name is used by family and friends. Next, a "town name" is given by parents, or the mission where the child was christened. Sometimes an employer gives it. The name is used in the outside world and is usually an English or Afrikaans name that is easier for non-Ndebele to use. Boys also have their praise names, which they invent themselves or which are given to them by their fellow initiates. Last is the "clan name," the name of the clan into which the person was born. That name is similar to the surname in the West.

The former Paramount Chief of the Ndzundza was named Mabusa Mabhogo David Mahlangu. From those four names we can guess that Mabusa was probably his traditional name, the one used at home by his family. Mabhogo was quite likely his praise name, given to him by his peers at initiation. (Mabhogo was the name of a famous early Ndzundza chief.) The next name, David, would be his town-name, easier for non-Ndebele to use. His last name, Mahlangu, would be his clan name. Generally, when you meet an Ndebele person, you will not immediately discover all the names that he or she uses.▲

chapter

6

KWANDEBELE: "THE PLACE OF THE NDEBELE"

THE SOUTH AFRICAN GOVERNMENT CREATED a homeland called KwaNdebele in 1979. Tens of thousands of Ndebele were resettled in that region from farms and other areas, meaning that they were forced to leave their homes to move there. This "resettlement" was a government policy that broke up existing communities to form another community.

For shelter, the people had to construct shacks of cardboard, tin, and sacks. Water had to be brought in by trucks. People with only farm skills and little schooling had a difficult time finding work in the new area. Some found low-paying jobs in Pretoria. But the commute from KwaNdebele took from four to six hours. The time needed for travel, work, and sleep left very little time for family life.

However, some Ndebele people supported the idea of KwaNdebele at first, hoping that it

APARTHEID HOMELANDS

Under South Africa's Apartheid government (1948–1994), the black ethnic groups of South Africa were forced to live in "homelands" and be ruled by black leaders appointed by the government. The Apartheid government's idea behind the homelands was that black people would be separated from white South Africa, where they could not vote and had no political rights, and that black people would also be separated according to ethnicity. In theory, each ethnic group would have its own country and leaders, but in fact South Africa's government controlled most of the important matters.

In this way, black people, who made up 87 percent of South Africa's population, were forced into ten ethnic homelands that made up only 13 percent of the land. Black people had once owned all the land; now they were forced into barren scraps of land where there were few jobs available.

To earn a living, migrant workers left the homelands to work in the big towns and cities of white South Africa, but they could never call these centers home. They could not settle permanently there; nor could they get permits for their families to join them. Although their labor contributed greatly to the wealth of white South Africa, they received practically no benefits.

The United Nations never recognized the "independent" homelands as separate countries. When South Africa became a democratic country in 1994, the homeland system was abolished.

would open up a new life for them. Some were tired of moving from one place to another and were happy to settle in a place they could call their own.

▼ RULERS OF KWANDEBELE ▼

According to various Ndebele, the rulers of the "homeland" were some Ndebele business-

people who wanted to take advantage of the white South African government's plan to make KwaNdebele a separate "independent" country. They hoped to get rich by taking new opportunities, so these businesspeople pushed KwaNdebele residents to support the plan for so-called independence. They had strong backing from the South African government.

By 1986, ordinary KwaNdebele people were upset and frightened by many of the activities happening around them. Vigilantes (people who take the law into their own hands, often violently) were terrorizing people. It became known that the chief minister of KwaNdebele and others in his administration had organized a vigilante group called Mbokotho ("grinding stone") to enforce their will. Hundreds of people fell victim to the Mbokotho, including schoolchildren. Many people who questioned or objected to decisions made by the KwaNdebele rulers were persecuted. There were ruthless kidnappings, beatings, and killings.

On one occasion, a high school principal called the police and the Mbokotho to come and discipline some of his pupils. Five police armored tanks and government vehicles arrived with members of the Mbokotho on board. The police teargassed and beat the pupils as they fled. Ten students and teachers were caught, tortured, and stabbed. Five teachers were released a

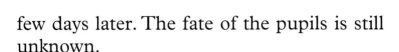

few days later. The fate of the pupils is still unknown.

On another occasion, a class staged a boycott because only certain pupils were eligible to receive free books. Carloads of armed vigilantes arrived. Many students were captured while fleeing and were tortured for two days. They reported receiving electric shocks and beatings on sensitive parts of their bodies. Another time, 380 men were abducted and forced to do balancing stunts on a floor covered with soapy water, and were whipped for slipping. Many were hospitalized, and a number died.

Violence was used against people of all ages suspected of criticizing the idea of "homeland independence" or the activities of the Mbokotho. Many other incidents occurred, including the murder of a student's father who supported the pupils' actions. People were outraged. The rulers of KwaNdebele said that only fifty mourners could attend this funeral, but thousands of people came anyway. Local buses were hijacked and rerouted to the funeral. The police and army fired teargas, birdshot, and rubber bullets at the mourners. The people resisted. Youths burned tires, shops, and houses belonging to Mbokotho members.

The youths then organized themselves to protect the ordinary Ndebele people against the Mbokotho. A large support group called the

Mass Democratic Movement became active. A leading section consisted of newly initiated young men (age sixteen to twenty) from KwaNdebele. They were joined by a group called the Comrades from the black townships of Pretoria. The Comrades were experienced in fighting oppression. They taught the young men of KwaNdebele how to organize and resist. They helped them plan strategy and showed them how to protect themselves. The Comrades explained even simple things, like how to stop the spread of teargas by dropping a plate over the canister.

One of the youth leaders who opposed the Mbokotho was the son of the chief minister. He said his father had "lost direction" and that promoting "homeland independence" was "misleading the Ndebele people into accepting the apartheid laws of Pretoria."

▼ END OF THE MBOKOTHO ▼

In July one of the Mbokotho leaders was killed by a car bomb. The bomber was never discovered. KwaNdebele's leaders realized that ordinary people were now fighting back. To calm things down, the KwaNdebele government outlawed the Mbokotho, but the KwaNdebele rulers continued to press for independence, ignoring the opposition from the people.

In desperation, the common people of

Chief Alfred Mabena, a supporter of "independence" for the homeland of Kwa-Ndebele, travels to a ceremony commemorating his wedding, wearing leopard skins associated with royalty (top). Seen below is the principal wife of Chief Mphezulu Jack Mahlangu admiring her baby son. Neither of these chiefs have the high rank of Paramount Chief David Mahlangu (now deceased), who eventually joined the majority of his people in opposing "independence." Today, the homeland system has been abolished, and the Ndebele may live wherever they please.

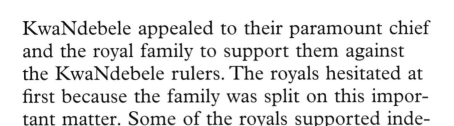

KwaNdebele appealed to their paramount chief and the royal family to support them against the KwaNdebele rulers. The royals hesitated at first because the family was split on this important matter. Some of the royals supported independence. But finally, the king and his family rallied behind the ordinary people.

A son of the paramount chief, Prince James Mahlangu, addressed the assembly of KwaNdebele representatives before they voted on whether or not KwaNdebele should accept independence. He said: "The people have sent me to tell the meeting that they were not consulted and will not accept independence, which they do not want. They are prepared to live peacefully without it." Many people who had packed into the public gallery cheered. Rejoicing and celebrating took place throughout KwaNdebele.

This was a striking example of the paramount chief's and the royal family's response to the will of the majority of their people.▲

chapter

7

TOWARD THE FUTURE

FROM APRIL 26 TO APRIL 29, 1994, SOME
22 million people voted in South Africa's first
democratic election that allowed people of all
races to vote. This signaled the end of white rule
and the hated systems of apartheid and "homelands." The Ndebele, along with all other South
Africans, have now become citizens of a free and
non-racist South Africa.

As a result of that historic election, Nelson
Mandela became South Africa's first black president. He set the tone for his new government
when he said: "We are starting a new era of
hope, of reconciliation, of nation-building."
President Mandela's political party, the African
National Congress, has committed itself to cor-
recting the many injustices blacks had suffered
under the apartheid system.

Rebuilding a divided country is not easy.
Many crucial steps have already been taken. One
was the adoption of the new constitution that
eliminated apartheid. Included was a Bill of
Fundamental Rights that ensures equal treat-

The Ndebele remain proud of their traditions, which are also enjoyed by others, such as tourists who buy dolls like those seen above. The Ndebele are now part of a united and democratic South Africa that is composed of people of many different ethnic backgrounds.

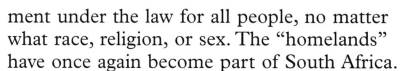

ment under the law for all people, no matter what race, religion, or sex. The "homelands" have once again become part of South Africa.

South Africans, including the Ndebele, now look forward to new opportunities. For example, South Africa can once again take part in world sports. Previously, sanctions had been placed against such participation. In 1995, South Africa won the World Cup in rugby. In February of 1996, the country won the Africa Cup in soccer. Then in August 1996 at the Olympic Games held in Atlanta, Josia Thugwane, an Ndebele from South Africa, became the first black South African ever to win an Olympic gold medal for his remarkable run in the men's marathon. Work came to a standstill at the South African coal mine where he is normally employed as a security guard. Everyone interrupted their work shifts to watch their hero on television and roared with jubilation at the finish.

South Africa's future looks promising. The Ndzundza Ndebele have shown strength throughout difficult times. Their unique painted houses were an important part of an era of struggle and resistance. Today, their deep pride in their identity, not only as Ndzundza Ndebele, but as an integrated part of the larger South Africa, remains. After their long struggle, these people are now an energetic, vibrant part of the new South Africa.▲

Glossary

Afrikaans Language of Boer settlers.

apartheid Political system in the Republic of South Africa (1948–1994) that separated people by race and allowed the white minority to rule the black majority.

Highveld A high, grassland plateau.

hlonipha To treat with respect; also, a secret language learned during initiation.

homeland A separate area where an ethnic group had to live.

imbongi A praise singer.

indentured laborer A person who is bound by contract to work for another for a specific amount of time.

ingoma Male initiation process.

izibongo The recitation of praise poems.

mace A decorated stick used in ceremonies.

poryana Neckpiece of initiated men.

sanction An economic and military measure used to punish a country for violating international law.

SAR South African Republic (1852–1902).

satirical Sarcastic; making fun of something or someone.

tribute To recognize another's superior power.

ubhutshulo A ceremonial staff.

wela Final stage of male initiation.

For Further Reading

Jeffery, David. "Ndebele People—Pioneers in Their Own Land." *National Geographic*, Vol. 169, No. 2, 1986.

McCaul, Colleen. *Satellite in Revolt.* Johannesburg: South African Institute of Race Relations, 1987.

Paton, Jonathan. *The Land and People of South Africa.* New York: J. B. Lippincott, 1990.

Powell, Ivor. *Ndebele.* Cape Town: Struik, 1995.

Saunders, Christopher C. *An Illustrated Dictionary of South African History.* Sandton, South Africa: Ibis Books and Editorial Services, 1994.

Schneider, Elizabeth Ann. "Art and Communication." In *African Art in Southern Africa,* edited by Anitra Nettleton and David Hammond-Tooke. Johannesburg: Ad. Donker, 1989.

Index

P

poryana (neckpieces), 43–44
Pretoria, 48, 51, 55
pride, 16, 19, 60

R

resettlement, forced, 51

S

Sotho language, 12, 15
South African Republic (SAR), 17, 18–19
Swaziland, 11

T

tenant laborers, 14
tourists, 22, 24
toys, 27–28

traditional dress, 11, 28, 32–36
Transvaal, 11, 16, 17, 19

U

ubhutshulo (ceremonial pole decorated with feathers), 31

W

war of 1883, 16–19, 31, 49
wela (final stage of initiation), 39–40

V

violence, 53–55

Z

zila (abstinence), 44, 45–46

ACKNOWLEDGMENTS

I would like to thank Dr. Chris Van Vuuren of the Anthropology Department of the University of South Africa, whose detailed studies of Ndzundza male initiation contributed a great deal to my research in Chapter 5. I would also like to thank Dr. Deborah James of the Social Anthropology Department at the University of the Witwatersrand who so kindly brought the above studies, and others, to my attention.

ABOUT THE AUTHOR

Elizabeth Ann Schneider has lived and worked for two years in Mozambique and for fourteen years in South Africa. Dr. Schneider has done and continues to do extensive research, field work, and photography throughout Africa. She received her Ph.D. from the University of the Witwatersrand in Johannesburg. Her dissertation "Paint, Pride, and Politics" is based upon her many years of research among the Ndebele people. She has also written numerous articles and reviews on southeastern African art.

CONSULTING EDITOR: Gary N. van Wyk, Ph.D.

PHOTO CREDITS: Elizabeth Ann Schneider, Ph.D.

LAYOUT AND DESIGN: Kim Sonsky